6. 1 mark
— The final section summarises the answers to some of the questions in the first paragraph.
OR 2 marks
— The opening paragraph asks a series of questions. The answers to these questions are summarised in the final section, which helps conclude the text for the reader.

Page 11 — Writer's Purpose Questions

1. 1 mark
— The writer wanted to make the reader wonder about the answers and want to read on.

2. 1 mark
— To show that the audience was impressed.
AND 1 mark
— To show that they did not expect the plane to fly.

3. 1 mark
— Yes — because these people changed lives.
OR 2 marks
— Yes — because it makes you realise that you don't need to have education or special training to invent something life-changing. Anyone with a good idea can be an inventor.

4. 1 mark
— To show that if you have an idea you should believe in it.
OR 2 marks
— To show that if famous inventors hadn't believed in their own inventions they'd never have been built, so if you have an idea you should believe in it.

5. 1 mark
— It shows that inventions can be simple.
AND 1 mark
— It shows that inventions can be very useful, and can even save people's lives.

The Gondrots

Page 16 — Inference Questions

1. 1 mark
— The quote means we know very little about our world and how everything works.

2. 1 mark
— The creature was relieved, because he knew he was going to be helped.
AND 1 mark
— The Morrisons were relieved, because they knew their television set was going to be fixed.

3. 1 mark
— Because people would not believe him.
AND 1 mark
— People might be shocked and frightened.

4. 1 mark
— It says in the story that Gondrots operate the TVs. They wouldn't do this unless they got on with inventors.
OR 2 marks
— The Gondrots get on well with inventors. The text says they have "worked together for years" and the relationship between Gondrots and inventors is described as "fantastic."

5. 1 mark for each suitable word, with an explanation
— Inquisitive — He went to find what was in the cellar.
— Clever — He tries to lure the Gondrots out with food.
— Timid — He is scared by his first sight of a Gondrot.

Page 17 — Writer's Purpose Q

1. 1 mark
— Because Edison was an inventor and the story is about inventors.
AND 1 mark
— To show the reader might find out some surprising things in the story.

2. 1 mark
introduce the main idea of the story

3. 1 mark
Funny — It is about funny characters.
OR 2 marks
Funny — It is about imaginary characters who look peculiar and do funny things.
OR 3 marks
Funny — It is about imaginary characters who look bizarre and have humorous names, e.g. Snizzel. The events in the story are also humorous, for example, the surprised reaction of Faraday on finding a Gondrot.

4. 1 mark
— It reminds the reader that the story is set in the past.

Pages 18/19 — Language Questions

1. 1 mark for underlining all three
screamed, dropped, ran

2. 1 mark
— The writer builds up suspense by not saying what is in the trap and by implying that it is something surprising.
AND 1 mark
— The suspense is built up with strong, descriptive words and phrases, e.g. "like a ghost", "powerful" and "slammed".

3. 1 mark
— The atmosphere in the room was scary and eerie.
AND 1 mark
— The room was very dark and the only light came from the candle.

4. 1 mark
— The reader pictures cold things such as ice and snow, which emphasises how white the Gondrot's skin is.

5. 1 mark
— To show how different it was when Faraday met the Gondrot.
OR 2 marks
— It adds humour by showing what would usually happen at such an important meeting, and then contrasting it with what actually happened.

6. 1 mark
— The first meeting between Faraday and Wesley wasn't a big occasion and it was a bit awkward.

7. 1 mark
— The writer wants to tell the reader how loud the sound seemed to the Gondrots.
AND 1 mark
— "Deafening" makes it sound loud enough to make the Gondrots go deaf for a while.

8. 1 mark
held his breath

9. 1 mark
— The character says the mousetrap tried to attack him.
OR 2 marks
— The character describes the mousetrap like a living thing, which attacked him and tried to swallow his foot.

Book 1

10. 1 mark
— The short sentence makes it seem like things are happening quickly.
AND 1 mark
— It emphasises how nervous Wesley is, which increases the tension.

Page 20 — Fact Retrieval Questions

1. 1 mark
Kicking the TV

2. 1 mark
Dust

3. 1 mark
— The Gondrot inside was feeling queasy and had fainted.

4. a) 1 mark
Through the plug in the socket.

b) 1 mark
A government trained Gondrot doctor.

5. 1 mark
Michael Faraday

Page 21 — Structure and Layout Questions

1. 1 mark for two or three correct
2 marks for all correct
3. Faraday is frightened by his first sight of a Gondrot.
4. Faraday learns about Latchett and feels guilty.
1. The Morrisons' television breaks down.
5. Faraday speaks to Wesley.
2. The repair man mends the TV.

2. 1 mark
— To build up excitement and make the secret of the Gondrots sound more impressive.

Page 21 — Context Questions

1. 1 mark
The Prologue is set after chapter 1.

AND 1 mark
— The family have a wide-screen TV, which hadn't been invented in 1812.

2. 1 mark for each
3 marks in total
— Fantasy creatures
— Unbelievable events — people not knowing about the creatures in their homes.
— TVs working differently to how they actually work in the real world.

The Wizard of Menlo Park

Pages 26/27 — Fact Retrieval Questions

1. 1 mark
Biography

2. 1 mark
'probably the world's greatest inventor.'

3. 1 mark
Phonograph

4. 1 mark
Time to do all he wanted to do.

5. 1 mark
that Edison invented things we still use today

6. 1 mark
1879

7. 1 mark
He lit up the streets outside his factory.

8. 1 mark
1400 patents

9. 1 mark for one correct answer
2 marks for all three correct
1891 — Invented the motion picture camera
Aged 13 — Set up his own newspaper
1879 — Moved to Menlo Park

10. 1 mark
The first motion picture camera.

11. 1 mark for each correct answer
1906-1931 — Tells us about the final years of Edison's life
Introduction — Builds up interest in the biography
1847-1877 — Tell us about Edison as a child
1877-1905 — Tells us about the busiest years of Edison's life

Page 28 — Structure and Layout Questions

1. 1 mark
— To separate them from the main story of Edison's life.
AND 1 mark
— They give the reader a more in-depth view of Edison's inventions and the impact they had.

2. 1 mark
— The subheading says what the text is about.
OR 2 marks
— The subheading summarises what the text is about, and also explains who the wizard of Menlo Park was.

3. 1 mark
— It does not need a glossary, as there are few difficult words in the text.
OR 2 marks
— It does not need a glossary as any difficult words like telegrapher or phonograph are explained. The 'Edison Facts' boxes explain things, so there's less need for a glossary.

4. 1 mark
— It sums up the points made in the introduction.
AND 1 mark
— This emphasises the main point of the text, to show what a great inventor Edison was.

5. 1 mark
— To make it easy to read.
AND 1 mark
— It divides the information into chunks, which makes it easier to remember.

Page 29 — Writer's Purpose Questions

1. 1 mark
creates interest by describing Edison as the world's greatest inventor.

2. 1 mark
— The writer thinks Edison was very intelligent.
AND 1 mark
— The writer thinks that our lives would be very different without Edison's useful inventions.

3. 1 mark
— Because Edison worked hard his whole life.
OR 2 marks
— Edison had some inspiration, but he also worked very hard.

OR 3 marks
— Although Edison had natural talent, he also worked very hard to make the most of it. It also shows Edison was not a show off, because he says the most important thing is hard work.

4. **1 mark**
— It makes the reader realise that Edison was a real person.
AND 1 mark
— It helps the reader to understand what Edison was like.
AND 1 mark
— The quotes add accurate historical evidence to the text.

Page 30 — Inference Questions

1. **1 mark for each correct answer**
Edison worked really hard from an early age.
Edison worked very long hours to achieve his success.

2. **1 mark**
— They thought his inventions were like magic.
AND 1 mark
— They were amazed by what he had invented.

3. **1 mark**
— He means it is obvious how good it is.
AND 1 mark
— It can play back voices, so it "speaks".

4. **1 mark**
— Because he invented lots of useful items.
OR 2 marks
— He patented over 1400 new inventions. Some of these have had a big impact on the way we live today, e.g. the electric light bulb and the movie camera.

Page 31 — Language Questions

1. **1 mark for underlining all three**
amazing, extraordinary, greatest.

2. **a) 1 mark for ticking the correct box**
The author
b) 1 mark
— It makes the reader feel like the writer is talking directly to them, so it makes the reader feel more involved.

3. **1 mark**
— The exclamation mark shows the writer can hardly believe Edison could produce a newspaper on a moving train.
AND 1 mark
— The exclamation mark shows the writer thinks the things that Edison did were amazing.

4. **1 mark**
— It helps the reader to imagine just how much of his time Edison spent inventing.
AND 1 mark
— It helps the reader to understand how single-minded Edison was.

Winds of Change

Page 36 — Inference Questions

1. **1 mark**
not listening to what people have to say

2. **1 mark**
— He has lived in the village a long time and wants to keep the countryside looking the same.

3. **1 mark**
— Because it will make life better for people in the village.

4. **1 mark**
— Angry
AND 1 mark
— He is angry because he doesn't want them spoiling his view or frightening his animals.

5. **1 mark**
— I think he is mainly concerned about himself rather than the environment.
AND 1 mark
— He is worried that his view will be spoiled and says it is "a very worrying time for me."

Page 37 — Language Questions

1. **1 mark**
— "Sleepy" suggests a peaceful village where very little happens.

2. **1 mark**
— Yes, because it draws the reader's attention by making it sound like there was a fight.
AND 1 mark
— The word 'clashes' is very dramatic and shows how strong the different opinions are.

3. **a) 1 mark**
— That he doesn't know much about wind turbines.
OR 2 marks
— That he doesn't know much about wind turbines, so his opinion shouldn't be taken too seriously.
b) 1 mark
— It sounds like the wind turbines are so ugly they will hurt your eyes.

4. **1 mark**
— 'Winds of Change' is a good title as the article is about a wind farm.
OR 2 marks
— 'Winds of Change' is a good title because the article is about wind farms and how the countryside might change as a result of them.
OR 3 marks
— 'Winds of Change' is a phrase meaning that big changes are coming. It is a good title because the article is about the differences a wind farm could make to the countryside and environment — as well as being a pun on "wind".

Page 38 — Fact Retrieval Questions

1. **1 mark**
— He thinks they are an eyesore and will frighten animals.

2. **1 mark**
— It will make pollution-free energy.

3. **1 mark for each**
— They will provide pollution-free energy.
— They will result in cleaner air in the village.
— They will attract tourists and bring money to the village.

4. **1 mark**
1888

5. **1 mark**
— He thinks it will bring money to the village as a tourist attraction.

6. **1 mark**
Over thirty

Book 1 / Book 2

Page 39 — Writer's Purpose Questions

1. **1 mark**
To show how inventions can upset communities.

2. **1 mark**
— To give a balanced argument.

3. **1 mark**
— To give the story some background.
AND 1 mark
— To make the reader realise that wind turbines have been around for a long time.

4. **1 mark**
— The writer is in favour of wind farms.

5. **1 mark**
— I think it is a fair, unbiased report overall.
OR 2 marks
— It is a fair report as it gives opinions of a selection of people and does not push the reader towards supporting one side over the other.
OR 3 marks
— It gives a range of different opinions, but might be slightly biased towards the wind farm. The concluding paragraph suggests that people aren't fully considering the impact of pollution if there isn't a wind farm.

The Whole Lot

Pages 40/41 — Questions On The Whole Lot

1. **1 mark**
The Wizard of Menlo Park

2. **1 mark**
Eureka!

3. **1 mark**
Winds of Change

4. **1 mark for one correct**
2 marks for all correct
The plans to develop the wind farm are yet to be fully decided but the local council welcomes the development.
— Newspaper article
As he gazed down at his catch with its petal white skin and its leaf-like hair, the creature opened its wide brown eyes.
— Fiction
He used the money he earned to buy more chemicals so he could continue his experiments.
— Biography

5. **1 mark for each correct answer**
Inform
Entertain
Give a balanced argument

6. **1 mark**
— They might show people that inventors are interesting and inspiring.
OR 2 marks
— The texts might make you realise how different life would be if it weren't for the work of inventors like the Wright brothers in 'Eureka!' and Edison in 'The Wizard of Menlo Park.'
OR 3 marks
— The texts might make you realise how different life would be if it weren't for the work of inventors, e.g. the Wright brothers inventing the aeroplane. The texts show that inventors like Edison were inspiring people. 'Eureka!' also suggests that you could become an inventor yourself.

7. **1 mark**
— 'The Gondrots', because I found it funny.
OR 2 marks
— 'The Gondrots', because it was entertaining. For example, I found it funny when the TV repairman turned out to be a government trained Gondrot doctor.
OR 3 marks
— 'The Gondrots' is my favourite because I found it entertaining. I liked the description, the humour and the imaginativeness of the writing. For example, I like the description of the Gondrots as having petal white skin and leaves for hair.

Book 2

> **N.B. A dash (—) before an answer means that it's just a suggestion.**
> *The wording of answers giving <u>facts</u> from the text can vary, so long as the fact is correct. For questions which ask for an <u>opinion</u> or <u>explanation</u> there's usually no 'correct' answer, but answers should be <u>based on the text</u> and go into a similar amount of <u>detail</u> to the sample answer.*

All About Boats

Page 8 — Structure and Layout Questions

1. **1 mark**
— To show each section contains separate information.

2. **1 mark**
— The important words are larger, so you'll read them first.

3. **1 mark**
— They show you what the different parts of the boat look like, and where they are.

4. **1 mark**
— They tell you what information you can expect to read.
OR 2 marks
— They tell you what information to expect and divide the writing into two chunks so it's easier to read.

5. **1 mark**
— Yes, it would show you what things look like.
OR 2 marks
— Yes. It would show you what the different things mentioned in the text look like, so it would be easier to understand what they are.

Page 9 — Inference Questions

1. **1 mark**
— A canoe does not weigh very much.

2. **1 mark**
— Cruise ships are powerful.
— A galleon is powerful.
OR 2 marks
— Cruise ships are very large so they need powerful engines to make them move.
— A galleon is powerful because its speed and cannons make it dangerous in battle.

3. **1 mark**
— Nowadays they have more equipment.
OR 2 marks
— In the past, sailors had to use simple tools like compasses. Nowadays they have more complicated gadgets like GPS.

Book 2

4. 1 mark
pinpoint

5. 1 mark
— Sailors in the past needed good knowledge of the stars so they could navigate at night.
AND 1 mark
— Modern sailors don't need this knowledge because they have gadgets (e.g. GPS) that allow them to navigate at night.

Pages 10/11 — Fact Retrieval Questions

1. 1 mark
Sails give them speed.

2. 1 mark
The front of the boat.

3. 1 mark
They use a compass.

4. 1 mark for one correct
2 marks for all correct
On lakes
On rivers
On sheltered coastlines

5. 1 mark for one correct
2 marks for all correct
Anchor — Heavy metal hook dropped to the sea bottom
Oar — Used to row the boat
Rudder — Used to steer the boat

6. 1 mark
Using a compass

7. 1 mark
The Sun
AND 1 mark
The stars

8. 1 mark for one correct
2 marks for all correct
Simple, easy to carry, light — Canoe
Huge, luxurious, comfortable — Cruise ship
Small, powerful, safety boat — Tug

9. 1 mark
At the back of the boat.

10. 1 mark
measure angles using the Sun

11. 1 mark
Global Positioning System

Page 12 — Language Questions

1. 1 mark
— To help the reader picture life at sea.
AND 1 mark
— To emphasise the first part of the sentence.

2. 1 mark
— It emphasises that compasses have been used for a long time.
OR 2 marks
— It emphasises that compasses have been used for a long time, and suggests the writer thinks they are more reliable than modern tools.

3. 1 mark
— To emphasise that it can pull big ships even though it's a small boat.

4. 1 mark
— Because the boat contains everything you might expect to find in a hotel.
AND 1 mark
— Because the boat floats on the water.

Page 13 — Writer's Purpose Questions

1. 1 mark
To introduce you to some types of boat and some sailing terms.

2. 1 mark
— To emphasise the fact that cruise ships are more like hotels than other boats.

3. 1 mark
— The galleon may sometimes need to escape from other ships.
OR 2 marks
— She wants to show that although galleons are good at fighting, they might need to get away from other ships if they are losing a battle.

4. 1 mark
— Navigators of the past.
OR 2 marks
— I think the writer has more admiration for navigators of the past as they used the Sun and stars to navigate, which needed more skill.
OR 3 marks
— The writer seems to admire navigators of the past who used simple tools like compasses and sextants. She calls a compass a "good, old-fashioned compass" which sounds like she likes it more. She suggests that modern tools might break down.

Jason and the Argonauts
Page 18 — Inference Questions

1. 1 mark
— Pelias is nasty. He puts Jason's father in prison.
OR 2 marks
— Pelias is proud and cowardly. He didn't want to fight Jason.
OR 3 marks
— Pelias is cunning because he tricks Jason into the challenge of fetching the fleece. He is also proud, as he won't hand the throne over to Jason without a challenge.

2. 1 mark
— Yes. He had the best sailors and a very good ship.
OR 2 marks
— Yes. He had the greatest warriors in his crew, including Heracles the strongest man. He also had a ship made from the best timber and blessed by the goddess Athene.

3. 1 mark
— Medea decided to help Jason as she heard her father being horrible to him.
OR 2 marks
— Medea wanted to help Jason because she had heard how "cruel and angry" her father had been to him. She felt sorry for him and decided to help.

Book 2

4. 1 mark for two correct
2 marks for all correct
Finds out his father is dead — Sorrow
Sees the sea boil by the Clashing Rocks — Fear
Challenged by his uncle Pelias — Anger
Starts to build his boat and gather his crew — Excitement

Page 19 — Structure and Layout Questions

1. 1 mark
— The author writes "if" like this to show Jason might refuse the challenge.
OR 2 marks
— The author writes "if" like this to make the reader think about whether Jason will accept the challenge. It emphasises the second part of the sentence — the condition that Pelias has put on Jason claiming the throne back.

2. 1 mark
— Because it tells the reader this is not the start of the full story.
OR 2 marks
— The writer has put the introduction of the story in italics as it shows that this part is important even though it isn't part of the full story.

3. 1 mark
— It shows you it's an exciting moment because Jason is shouting.
OR 2 marks
— It makes you imagine Jason shouting loudly and adds to the sense of urgency and excitement.

4. 1 mark
— It helps the reader understand the story.
OR 2 marks
— It helps the reader understand what is going on by giving the story context.

Pages 20/21 — Language Questions

1. 1 mark
marched
AND 1 mark
declared

2. 1 mark
— The introduction summarises the main points about Jason's history, it doesn't include details.

3. 1 mark
— The paragraph builds tension through describing the scene in detail.
OR 2 marks
— The author uses lots of descriptive words and phrases to help the reader paint a picture of what is happening, for example, "rumbling", "seething" and "like a sword."
OR 3 marks
— The author creates a strong atmosphere with the picture of Orpheus singing at the stern "over the rumbling thunder" and the *Argo* cutting through the water "like a sword." She doesn't say whether the *Argo* escaped till the last few words.

4. 1 mark
— Because the dragon moved quickly.
OR 2 marks
— The dragon moved quickly and sharply. The word "lunged" sounds more frightening than "moved" or "went".

5. 1 mark
— Jason sprang back
OR
— Jason climbed softly

6. 1 mark
— To make them sound more mysterious.
OR 2 marks
— To make them sound more mysterious and magical and to show that only Medea knew them.

7. 1 mark
— as soon as their feet touched the deck
OR
— ran for the harbour

8. 1 mark
— The sea started to bubble like in a storm.
OR 2 marks
— It means the sea is bubbling and frothing as if in a storm. This helps the reader to imagine how the sea looked.

9. 1 mark
— These verbs make the dragon sound angry and intimidating.
OR 2 marks
— These verbs sound like the noises the dragon is making, so it helps the reader to imagine how intimidating the dragon is.

Pages 22/23 — Fact Retrieval Questions

1. 1 mark
The Centaurs

2. 1 mark
Phineas

3. 1 mark
Jason learnt hunting, sailing and history.

4. 1 mark
— The goddess Athene blessed the ship.

5. 1 mark
an old oak tree

6. 1 mark
Pelion

7. 1 mark for one correct
2 marks for all correct
5 — The Argonauts escape from Colchis with the Golden Fleece.
4 — Jason escapes the Clashing Rocks.
2 — Jason builds a fine boat called the *Argo*, which is blessed by Athene.
3 — Phineas tells Jason how to defeat the Clashing Rocks.

8. 1 mark
— he began to prepare for the perilous voyage

9. 1 mark
The twins, Castor and Pollux

Page 23 — Context Question

1. 1 mark for each suggestion
3 marks in total
— Magic
— Goddesses
— Mythical creatures
— A quest
— Legendary characters like Heracles

Book 2

The Kon-Tiki Voyage

Page 28 — Writer's Purpose Questions

1. 1 mark
— To show the reader it took a long time.
OR 2 marks
— It is factual and informs the reader of the timescale of events. It also increases the impression of how long and difficult the journey was.

2. 1 mark
— No, I do not feel the stories are strong enough evidence, as they have no facts to support them.
OR 2 marks
— I don't feel the stories are strong enough evidence as they are both from folklore and happened so long ago that there are hardly any facts to back them up.

3. 1 mark
— 'The Kon-Tiki Voyage' helps the reader understand what happened, before explaining why it happened in 'Two Ancient Journeys'.
OR 2 marks
— 'The Kon-Tiki Voyage' informs the reader that it's possible to travel across the Pacific Ocean on a simple raft. 'Two Ancient Journeys' then goes on to explain to the reader why Thor Heyerdahl believed that Kon-Tiki had made the voyage.

4. 1 mark
— To make the reader think about what they have read.

Page 29 — Inference Questions

1. 1 mark
Because he was defeated by a cruel tribe of warriors.

2. 1 mark
— The crew members will have lots of different memories of the journey.
OR 2 marks
— The crew had a memorable journey about which they might have mixed feelings — as well as beautiful sights there were also dangers.

3. 1 mark
— 'Two Ancient Journeys' is a good title as it clearly explains what the reader is about to read without giving too much away.

4. 1 mark
— I don't think Thor Heyerdahl knew what lay ahead or how tough it would be.
OR 2 marks
— I think that Thor Heyerdahl did not expect the journey to be as difficult as it was. The article says that the crew had "no idea" how difficult the journey would be.
OR 3 marks
— I don't think Thor Heyerdahl expected it to be so difficult. He knew that he was embarking on a long voyage in a simple raft, but he believed it was possible to "survive". The text says that the crew had "no idea how long the journey would take, or how difficult it would be."

Page 30 — Language Questions

1. 1 mark
as though they were sailing amongst the stars

2. 1 mark
— Because it was a big, violent battle.
OR 2 marks
— Because it was a big, violent battle and is important in the story.

3. 1 mark
— That it is a legend from ancient times.

4. 1 mark
battered

5. 1 mark
— The crew felt like they were sailing through the night sky, because the fish around them were glittering like stars.
OR 2 marks
— As the night and the sea were dark, the glowing creatures made the crew feel like they were sailing through the sky. This shows how some things they saw were beautiful and made the journey worthwhile.

Page 31 — Structure and Layout Questions

1. 1 mark
— Because each box is about a separate journey.

2. 1 mark
— Because "The Kon-Tiki Voyage" is the main heading and "Two Ancient Journeys" is a subheading.

3. 1 mark
— Subheadings let the reader know that the next section of writing will discuss a different part of the topic.

4. 1 mark
— It makes you realise how far they travelled.
OR 2 marks
— The map helps you as it gives you an idea of the length of the journey and why it took the crew so long. It also reminds you of where the places mentioned in the text are geographically.

5. 1 mark for each suggestion
2 marks in total
— A picture of the raft to give an idea of what they travelled on.
— A picture of Thor Heyerdahl to help the reader picture him on the voyage.
— Photos taken on the voyage, e.g. of the flying fish.

6. 1 mark for one suggestion
— By using bullet points.
— By using bold text for important words.
— By underlining or italicising important words.

Pages 32/33 — Fact Retrieval Questions

1. 1 mark for each correct answer
3 marks altogether
Storms
Shark attacks
Falling overboard

2. 1 mark
— 3 months and 10 days
OR
— from 28 April to 7 August

3. 1 mark
there are many stories
OR
The stories say

Book 2

4. **1 mark for two correct**
   2 marks for all correct
   <u>When did the expedition begin?</u> — April 28 1947
   When was the expedition leader? — <u>Thor Heyerdahl</u>
   How many people went? — <u>Six</u>
   <u>When did it end?</u> — August 7 1947

5. **1 mark**
   East

6. **1 mark**
   Tall and pale skinned

7. **1 mark**
   The voyage of *Kon-Tiki*

8. **1 mark**
   The original Kon-Tiki journey

9. **1 mark for one correct**
   2 marks for all correct
   Thor Heyerdahl — captain
   Kon-Tiki — king
   Tiki — chief

10. **1 mark**
    Big statues carved out of rock.

Raising a Storm

Pages 38/39 — Fact Retrieval Questions

1. **1 mark**
   Raise it and turn it into a floating museum.

2. **1 mark**
   10th April 1912

3. **1 mark**
   11.45pm, Sunday April 14th 1912

4. **1 mark**
   Marlene Lenit

5. **1 mark for each correct answer**
   2 marks in total
   It sailed from Southampton.
   Its destination was New York.

6. **1 mark**
   Respect The *Titanic*

7. **1 mark**
   — They see it as an insult to the memories of those who died.

8. **1 mark**
   with containers of pressurised air

9. **1 mark**
   The governments of the countries that the victims of the tragedy came from.

10. **1 mark for each correct tick**
    2 marks in total
    The victims' families feel strongly about protecting their memory.
    Many artefacts are still lying at the bottom of the Atlantic.

Pages 40/41 — Writer's Purpose Questions

1. **1 mark**
   — It tells you Jose Allaz's plans for raising the *Titanic*.

2. **1 mark**
   — To give both sides of the argument.
   AND 1 mark
   — To make sure the article is unbiased.

3. **1 mark**
   — His quotes are put in first because he is the one putting the plans forward and starting the controversy.

4. **1 mark**
   — Marlene Lenit was an eyewitness of the tragic event and so her views about what should happen are important.

5. **1 mark**
   — Yes, it is a balanced argument as it gives points for and against.
   OR 2 marks
   — It is a balanced argument because it describes both points of view, and includes interviews with people from both sides of the argument. It allows the reader to decide what they think.
   OR 3 marks
   — It is a balanced argument because it describes and quotes different points of view but doesn't criticise any of them or try to persuade the reader that one is right. This allows the reader to make their own opinion.

6. **1 mark**
   — Because it is giving a strong opinion and would make the reader want to carry on reading.
   OR 2 marks
   — It is a subheading giving a taste of what the article is about. This quote gives the idea that this article is going to contain strong opinions and be interesting to read.

7. **1 mark**
   — The writer uses the final paragraph to say how they think it will end.
   OR 2 marks
   — The writer uses the last paragraph to say that no decision has been made and to give their opinion of what they think will happen — the plans will be rejected as a mark of respect for the victims.

8. **1 mark**
   — I would not like to go to the museum as I think it would be too scary to be in the middle of the Atlantic.
   OR 2 marks
   — I don't think I would feel comfortable in the museum as I think it would be disrespectful to the people who had died on the ship.

9. **1 mark**
   — Yes, the writer shows he is being thoughtless by not considering those who died on the *Titanic* and their relatives.
   OR 2 marks
   — The article makes us think Jose Allaz is being thoughtless as it shows he doesn't consider the feelings of survivors like Marlene Lenit, who don't want to remember the "horrific night". He seems to view the museum solely as a way of making money.

Page 42 — Language Questions

1. a) **1 mark**
   — It makes you wonder what the plans are.
   OR 2 marks
   — This opening raises lots of questions and makes it sound as if something dramatic ("a storm") is about to happen. It makes you wonder what the "controversial plans" are and makes you want to read on.

   b) **1 mark**
   — Because a storm can be used to describe an argument, but is also makes people think of the sea.

2. **a) 1 mark**
— People have cherished memories of those that died when the ship sank and feel that they should be allowed to remain undisturbed.
   b) 1 mark
— The wreck is going to be raised, which some people think is disrespectful to the dead on the ship, all because Allaz wants to make money.

3. **1 mark**
— It means the adults on the sinking ship needed help as well.
   OR 2 marks
— It means the grown-ups needed help too but didn't get it. This makes you realise how frightening the events on board the Titanic really were.

Page 43 — Inference Questions

1. **1 mark**
— Because it was the largest ship ever built and used the "latest technology".

2. **1 mark for each suggestion**
   3 marks in total
— greedy
— excited
— adventurous
— selfish

3. **1 mark**
— Señor Allaz is not sympathetic to the victims because he wants to raise the *Titanic*.
   OR 2 marks
— Señor Allaz is not really sympathetic towards the victims as he is more interested in "making back the money".

4. **1 mark**
— As a mark of respect for the dead.
   OR 2 marks
— All of the governments of those who died have to agree to the boat being raised. The writer doesn't think this will happen because of respect for the dead.

5. **1 mark**
— She doesn't want the plans to go ahead.
   AND 1 mark
— She doesn't want there to be a reminder of that night as it was terrifying.

The Whole Lot

Pages 44/45 — Questions On The Whole Lot

1. **1 mark for one correct**
   2 marks for all correct
It is an insult to the memories of the brave and tragic souls that perished. — Newspaper article
Around the oak's trunk a dragon lay twisted in thousands of coils. — Fiction
Nowadays, ships use fancy electronic devices to tell them exactly where they are. — Non-fiction

2. **1 mark**
All About Boats

3. **1 mark**
Raising a Storm

4. **1 mark**
— She wanted to show what it is like living with boats and highlight how important they are.

5. **1 mark**
— It tells the reader why she thinks sea travel is important and why she has included the different articles.

6. **1 mark**
— Yes, because it helps us to understand why the book was written.
   OR 2 marks
— Yes, it explains why the book was put together and gives a summary of each article.
   OR 3 marks
— Yes, it explains why the book was put together and shares the editor's enthusiasm for the subject with the reader. It also summarises the different articles and lets us know what to expect.

7. **1 mark**
— I found 'The Kon-Tiki Voyage' the best as it gave us information about the dangers the sailors faced.
   OR 2 marks
— 'The Kon-Tiki Voyage' was the most interesting as it told an exciting story as well as interesting myths. 'All About Boats' was very factual and less interesting.

8. **No marks for circling a title.**
   1 mark
— 'Jason and the Argonauts' was best because it tells an exciting story.
   OR 2 marks
— 'Jason and the Argonauts' was best because it tells an exciting story with magic, adventure and imaginative ideas like the Clashing Rocks.

Book 3

> **N.B. A dash (—) before an answer means that it's just a suggestion.**
> *The wording of answers giving <u>facts</u> from the text can vary, so long as the fact is correct. For questions which ask for an <u>opinion</u> or <u>explanation</u> there's usually no 'correct' answer, but answers should be <u>based on the text</u> and go into a similar amount of <u>detail</u> to the sample answer.*

Saved?

Pages 4/5 — Inference Questions

1. **1 mark**
death

2. **1 mark**
bullets

3. **1 mark**
they had been killed by humans

4. **1 mark**
— hunting prey

5. **1 mark**
— No, because he knows that his ancestors have died and that one day he will die too.
   OR 2 marks
— No, because he accepts that dying is a natural part of life and it will happen to all animals one day.

6. **1 mark**
— unhappy
— confused

Book 3

7. 1 mark
— strong
— unfamiliar
— frightening

8. 1 mark
"sacred cycle of life"

9. 1 mark
human children

10. 1 mark
— The sound of the waterfall was similar to the roars of its brothers, making the creature confused.

11. 1 mark
Proud to be born free and living free
AND 1 mark
Angry and confused and lonely

Pages 6/7 — Inference Questions

1. 1 mark
Then Man came.

2. 1 mark
a lion
AND 1 mark
— it roars
— it hunts
— use of word "cubs"

3. 1 mark
— The lion wants to be at home and doesn't want to be in a cage.
OR 2 marks
— The people have rescued the lion from the dangers of the Serengeti, but the lion would rather be there than in the unfamiliar safety of the cage.

4. 1 mark
— The lion thought it was dead.
OR 2 marks
— The lion thought it had been killed and believed it would meet up with its dead relatives in an afterlife.

5. 1 mark
The creature was shot with drugs that knocked it out.

6. 1 mark
The darkness was swift for my victims.

7. 1 mark
— Life has not followed the pattern that the lion expected and that it thinks is natural.
OR 2 marks
— The lion is surprised because men have arrived in the Serengeti and are killing the lions — which isn't part of the natural way of life that the lion is used to.
OR 3 marks
— The lion is confused because it expected to live the same life as its ancestors, as a predator in the Serengeti. Instead the lions have become prey and are killed by poachers — "My brothers became the victims." The lion is shocked by man's arrival and actions.

8. 1 mark
— The lion doesn't like humans because they killed its relatives and put it in a zoo.
OR 2 marks
— The lion doesn't like humans as they killed its brothers and locked it up in a cage. It blames the humans for changing the way of life the lions had in the Serengeti, as everything changed after "Man came".

9. 1 mark
— In the first verse the victims are the lion's prey and in the second verse the lions become the victims of man.
OR 2 marks
— In the first verse the victims are the lion's prey but in the second verse the lions become the victims as man comes and kills them. The victims in the first verse feel "no anger" because their death is part of the "sacred cycle", but the death of the lions is "unnatural".

Page 8 — Fact Retrieval Questions

1. 1 mark
proud

2. 1 mark
they knew a sacred cycle of life had been completed

3. 1 mark
a silent man-cage of steel

4. 1 mark for each correct answer
searched
sought
hunted

5. 1 mark for one of the following
— I am a proud, proud beast from the Serengeti
— Then Man came

6. 1 mark for each correct answer
The stripes in the sunlit reeds.
The stripes of metal.

Page 9 — Writer's Purpose Questions

1. 1 mark
— It shows the reader that the lion could smell a strange scent, so it must be somewhere unfamiliar.
OR 2 marks
— Describing the smells like this helps the reader imagine how uncomfortable ("heavy") and strange ("foreign") it must be for the lion.

2. 1 mark
— It links the end back to the start so it sounds complete.
OR 2 marks
— It links the end to the start and reminds us how much has changed but that the lion is still the same.

3. a) 1 mark
Sad

b) 1 mark
— The lion expects to meet up with his ancestors, but instead wakes to find himself in an unfamiliar place.
OR 2 marks
— The line "I hoped to be greeted by ancestors" shows that the lion hopes to be in the afterlife, but instead he is in a cage with people staring at him. This makes you feel sorry for him.

4. 1 mark
— The author doesn't like animals being captured and put in a zoo.
OR 2 marks
— The author doesn't like animals being captured and put in a zoo because it changes the natural cycle. The author believes that animals should be in their natural environment.

Book 3

OR 3 marks
— Phrases like "What unnatural cycle was this?" show that the author thinks lions should be left in their natural environment. The author also shows that the animals themselves would rather be in their natural environment, with the line "how I wish I was still there."

Pages 10/11 — Language Questions

1. **1 mark for each up to 2 marks**
    swift, silent, poison

2. **1 mark for each of the following**
    deceived, tricked, fooled

3. **1 mark**
    — Darkness is often used to describe death.
    OR 2 marks
    — Darkness is a good word to use to describe death as it makes us think of night or sleep. Death is sometimes described as a long sleep.

4. **1 mark**
    — The movement of a hunting lion can be described as a prowl.
    OR 2 marks
    — Prowled is a good word to use to describe the hunting lion as it helps the reader to picture the creature moving silently and stealthily towards its prey.

5. **1 mark**
    — The poem starts with the lion hunting and capturing animals, and ends with the lion being hunted and captured.
    OR 2 marks
    — The contrasts in the poem tell the story of the lion changing from being a "proud beast" who hunts for prey, into a creature who is hunted and captured.
    OR 3 marks
    — The poem contrasts two very clear pictures of the lion to tell its story. The first is the "proud" and powerful lion, ruler of the Serengeti. The second is the confused and uneasy lion, who has become the property of man.

6. **1 mark**
    — The author uses "stripes" as the bars of the cage are vertical, like stripes.
    OR 2 marks
    — The bars are vertical and look like stripes. The idea of stripes is familiar from the Serengeti (e.g. the reeds in the second verse) so it shows how the lion might view the bars.

7. **1 mark**
    — The author uses "Cold grey dust" to highlight the fact that the lion is away from its habitat.
    OR 2 marks
    — The author uses "Cold grey dust" to show the contrast of the conditions the lion is now in with the safe "dusty bones and dirt of my ancestors" of the Serengeti.

8. **1 mark**
    — In the poem the lion isn't really saved.
    OR 2 marks
    — In the poem, men take the lion to a zoo, probably to save it from the dangers of poachers. The lion doesn't feel that it has been saved though, as it doesn't like the zoo.
    OR 3 marks
    — In the poem, men try to save the lion from the dangers of the wild by putting it in a zoo. However, the lion would prefer the dangers to life in a cage: "But now I am saved from it – how I wish I was still there."

9. **1 mark**
    — Lots of things happen in a short time so the pace of the poem is quicker here than in previous parts of the poem.
    OR 2 marks
    — The pace of the poem speeds up here because the sentences are shorter so a lot happens in a few lines. This highlights the lion's frantic searching.

Walking With Hunters
Pages 16/17 — Inference Questions

1. **1 mark**
    — They are camping.

2. **1 mark**
    — It had been a proud animal in life, but it had an ugly death when it was killed by a poacher.
    OR 2 marks
    — The animal lived a proud life but it had a sad death when killed by a poacher. The whole point of the journey is to save rhinos from this kind of death.

3. **1 mark**
    four-wheel drive pick-up trucks

4. **1 mark**
    — She felt in high "spirits".
    OR 2 marks
    — She felt excited and full of "anticipation". She also says "spirits were high" as they set off.

5. **1 mark**
    — She was happy to see the rhinos in their habitat.
    OR 2 marks
    — She feels very happy as she can see the beauty of the rhino in the comfortable, familiar surroundings of its homeland.

6. **1 mark**
    — That it's a life full of fear of poachers, and that all they can think about is "their own survival".

7. **1 mark**
    — She saw the badness of the poachers and the goodness of the conservationists.
    OR 2 marks
    — Anne has mixed feelings. She was sad at the "cruelty" of the poachers but also proud of the bravery of people on the expedition who "fight against the same cruelty".

8. **1 mark**
    — The rhino's journey to Kenya.
    OR 2 marks
    — The journey the rhino will make first to Kenya and then on to "her part in the recovery of the species".

9. **1 mark**
    — She had helped rescue Marilyn.
    OR 2 marks
    — She had seen the rhino being rescued and played a small part in protecting the rhino species.

10. **1 mark**
    — That it's very cruel and is putting animals in danger.

Book 3

1. **1 mark**
   my heart was pounding

2. **1 mark**
   — Because it is a new day.
   OR 2 marks
   — Because the dawn brings a new day and starts everything once again, like it is newly-born.

3. **1 mark**
   — Because the truck hopped around on the uneven ground like a kangaroo.

4. **1 mark**
   — It shows the importance of what is about to happen.

5. **1 mark**
   — The truck moved fast.
   OR 2 marks
   — The truck moved off very quickly and urgently.

6. **1 mark**
   — It helps us to picture the rhino's skin.
   OR 2 marks
   — It helps us to picture what the rhino's skin looks like and shows us how strong it is.

7. **1 mark**
   — Yes, because the author is on a journey with people who hunt for wild animals.
   OR 2 marks
   — Yes, because it describes how Anne felt when they were tracking the rhinos. It was a kind of hunting expedition, even though they weren't trying to kill the animals, but save them.

8. **a) 1 mark**
   Clinging, yellow
   b) 1 mark
   — The sandy dust created by the running rhinos and the trucks going after them.
   OR 2 marks
   — Dry dust churned up by the trucks and by the running rhinos, which hovers in the air like clouds.

9. **1 mark**
   — It is a beautiful creature that did not deserve to die.
   OR 2 marks
   — It is a beautiful creature that should be saved, not killed. The description makes us feel sad that it has been killed.

10. **1 mark**
    — Anne le Trimel is shaking because she's so angry about what other humans have done to the rhino.
    OR 2 marks
    — Anne le Trimel is so angry and full of shame at the terrible thing that humans have done to the rhino, that she is shaking because she can't control her emotions.

Page 20 — Fact Retrieval Questions

1. **1 mark**
   Marilyn

2. **1 mark each for any two**
   — bucking
   — snorting
   — tussling

3. **1 mark**
   to be part of a breeding programme

4. **1 mark**
   To help save a black rhino from poachers.

5. **1 mark**
   — They can shoot bullets to kill the rhinos.
   AND 1 mark
   — They can shoot darts which tranquillise the rhinos so that they can be moved to a safer place.

Page 21 — Writer's Purpose Questions

1. **1 mark**
   — She makes you feel sad because she says it was "the saddest thing I had ever seen in my life".
   OR 2 marks
   — She makes you feel sad because she describes the rhino as "perfect" apart from where it's horn has been ripped off. She also makes you feel angry as the rhino has just been left to "rot in the dust".

2. **1 mark**
   — Because she wanted to show the reader that it was morning and everything was quiet.
   OR 2 marks
   — Because she felt so relaxed and comfortable and this makes a big contrast with what happens later in the expedition.
   OR 3 marks
   — Because at the beginning of the expedition she felt so relaxed and comfortable. This contrasts well with what happens later, which makes the diary more dramatic. The next day she describes that her "heart was pounding".

3. **1 mark**
   — To tell us how she moved from place to place.
   OR 2 marks
   — To help the reader understand what if felt like to be there. For example, the word "kangarooed" makes you think of being bounced around.
   OR 3 marks
   — To set the scene and to help the reader imagine what it was like to be there. For example, the phrase "kangarooed our way" helps to add to the excitement of the description of the start of the expedition.

4. **1 mark**
   — She thinks it is cruel and it makes her sad.
   OR 2 marks
   — She thinks poaching is cruel. She says it makes her sad that "People like poachers who kill for profit are capable of such cruelty".
   OR 3 marks
   — She thinks poaching is cruel. She describes when she sees the rhino that has been killed by the poachers as "the saddest thing I had ever seen in my life". She also says it makes her sad to think people are "capable of such cruelty".

Born Free?

Page 26 — Structure and Layout Questions

1. **1 mark**
   — To show the different events over a period of time.
   OR 2 marks
   — The three sections contain information about zoos from three different periods of history.

2. **1 mark**
   — This is separate information about the author, which wouldn't fit into the information about the history of zoos.

Book 3

3. 1 mark
— The titles tell you the time period the box covers.

4. 1 mark
— The glossary helps you with words you might not understand.
OR 2 marks
— The glossary picks out words you may find difficult and explains them in a way you can understand. This makes the text easier to read.

5. 1 mark for one correct
2 marks for all correct
2 — Ancient Greeks collected birds
3 — A polar bear and an elephant sent to the Tower of London
4 — Paying guests can visit the animals in the Tower of London

Page 27 — Writer's Purpose Questions

1. 1 mark
— To give facts about the history of zoos.

2. 1 mark
introduces the main points of the text

3. a) 1 mark
Animal lovers

b) 1 mark
— The text tells the history of zoos.
OR 2 marks
— It helps the reader to understand the development of zoos and how they help "the survival of some of the world's rarest creatures".

4. 1 mark
— To make the reader think that scientists should have thought of using zoos to study animals sooner.

Pages 28/29 — Fact Retrieval Questions

1. 1 mark
for over 2500 years

2. 1 mark
1800s

3. 1 mark
The Ancient Greeks

4. 1 mark
The early 1990s

5. 1 mark
the history of animal collections and zoos

6. 1 mark
— Through Egyptian hieroglyphics
OR
— Through old Greek paintings and carvings
OR
— Written evidence from Roman times

7. 1 mark
improved due to new ideas and laws

8. 1 mark for each correct answer
• 1200s — Animal collection started at the Tower of London by King John I.
• 1700s — Paying guests invited to the Tower to see the exhibits for the first time.
• 1800s — The Zoological Society of London opens the London Zoological Gardens.

9. 1 mark for one correct
2 marks for all correct
In the Middle Ages they — kept animals in the Tower of London
The Greeks — had large public collections of wild birds
Zoos today — keep animals to protect them from extinction

Pages 30/31 — Inference Questions

1. 1 mark
— Some points will surprise the reader.
OR 2 marks
— Some of the facts will surprise you, e.g. that the Egyptians kept wild animals.

2. 1 mark
— They were probably the most impressive and unusual animals to go to the Tower.

3. 1 mark
— There are now laws to make sure they are looked after properly.
OR 2 marks
— They used to be kept to show off but now they are kept for conservation. There are also laws in place to make sure they are looked after properly.

4. 1 mark
To discover more about animals.

5. 1 mark
— Yes. Even though he kept animals in the Tower of London, he tried to improve their living conditions.

6. 1 mark
— She doesn't like them.
OR 2 marks
— The "just to show off their wealth" part tells us that the author thinks that the Romans were wrong to use animals only to demonstrate their wealth.

Page 31 — Context Questions

1. 1 mark
— There is more evidence available about recent times. It is more difficult to find correct information from longer ago.

2. 1 mark each
Contains facts
Based on reality

Roll Up! Roll Up!
Pages 34/35 — Fact Retrieval Questions

1. 1 mark
Fair Play For Animals

2. 1 mark each
Demonstrate outside the circus
Show video evidence of circus animals suffering on TV

3. 1 mark each
The animals are kept in cramped cages
The animals are starved and beaten

4. 1 mark
— He has introduced new animals.

5. 1 mark
— He would have to sell them.

6. 1 mark
— He might get caught by inspectors and his circus would be shut down.

Book 3

7. 1 mark
Jan-Eric Rubensson

8. 1 mark
cruel to animals

9. 1 mark
— He thinks it's popular because people get to see animals up close.
OR 2 marks
— He thinks circuses are popular as they allow people to "see these things" which they don't usually see.

10. 1 mark each
The circus opens on Tuesday 18 June
The circus has been in operation for over fifty years

11. 1 mark
— That people in Britain "approve of this kind of torture."

Page 36 — Inference Questions

1. 1 mark
angry and concerned
AND 1 mark
— He describes the events in the circus as "horrific and barbaric" and he wants this to stop.

2. 1 mark
— He doesn't really care what other people think about him as they are likely to think something bad whatever he does.

3. 1 mark
A threat

4. 1 mark
— Yes, the government wants the circus to go ahead.
OR 2 marks
— The government wants the circus to go ahead. They don't want to upset "European relations", so they won't stop the circus without "further conclusive evidence".

Page 37 — Structure and Layout Questions

1. 1 mark for all correct
A — Headline
B — Subheading
C — Summary of article
D — Caption

2. 1 mark
— To make it stand out from the rest of the article.
OR 2 marks
— To make it stand out and advertise that there will be more on the story on Saturday so people will buy the newspaper then.

3. 1 mark each for any two
— The text is divided into columns.
— The text is split into short paragraphs.
— The headline is in a large bold font.
— The subheading is in white on a black background to make it stand out.

The Whole Lot

Pages 39/40/41 — Questions On The Whole Lot

1. 1 mark
'Born Free?'

2. 1 mark
'Roll Up! Roll Up!'

3. 1 mark
'Walking With Hunters'

4. 1 mark for one correct
2 marks for all correct
'Roll Up! Roll Up!' — Argument about a circus
'Saved?' — Poem from an animal's point of view
'Born Free?' — Facts about the history of zoos
'Walking With Hunters' — Account of an expedition to catch a rhino

5. 1 mark for one correct
2 marks for all correct
Entertainment, balanced argument, opinion

6. 1 mark for one correct
2 marks for all correct
A rhino was lying dead on the ground. — 'Walking With Hunters'.
Many Chinese emperors had large collections of animals. — 'Born Free?'
The demonstrators will camp outside and stop people from getting in. — 'Roll Up! Roll Up!'
My brothers were nowhere to be found. — 'Saved?'

7. 1 mark for one correct
2 marks for all correct
In the late 1990s, a zoo keeper who didn't give his animals enough food couldn't be prosecuted. — False
Poachers kill rhinos just for their skins — their horns aren't very valuable. — False
Zoos are only for people's entertainment. — False
People who are proved to have mistreated animals are punished. — True
A lion probably wouldn't notice if it was taken from its natural habitat and put in a cage in a zoo. — False

8. 1 mark
'Born Free?'

9. 1 mark
'Saved?'

10. 1 mark
— The poem describes what it's like living in a cage.
OR 2 marks
— The poem helps you to understand why the design changed from cages to open pens by illustrating the distress an animal may experience when they are kept in a cage.

11. 1 mark for one correct
2 marks for all correct
'Saved?' — Bad
'Walking With Hunters' — Both
'Born Free?' — Both
'Roll Up! Roll Up!' — Bad

ISBN 978 1 84146 486 2

9 781841 464862

E6A22

Contributor: Russ Brown.